The Lost Shimmer

Written by Chitra Soundar

Illustrated by Debasmita Dasgupta

Collins

Reese lived with her friends in a valley.
Her friends noticed that she looked gloomy.

"Fly with us," her friends called. But Reese could
not glow and shimmer like them.

"Not until I'm able to shimmer when I fly," Reese replied.

Reese headed to the woods to find her glow.

Some snowdrops called out gently, "Have our snowy white petals."

Reese thanked them.

That night, Reese still didn't glow.

But she didn't give up.

From the huge swirling sea, some kitefin sharks called, "Have our blue-white shimmer."

Reese thanked the kindly sharks.

Reese still didn't glow.

But she didn't give up.

The giant moon glowed in the sky.

"Maybe the icy moon will give some of its shimmer to me," whispered Reese.

Reese spread her wings and headed through the silvery clouds.

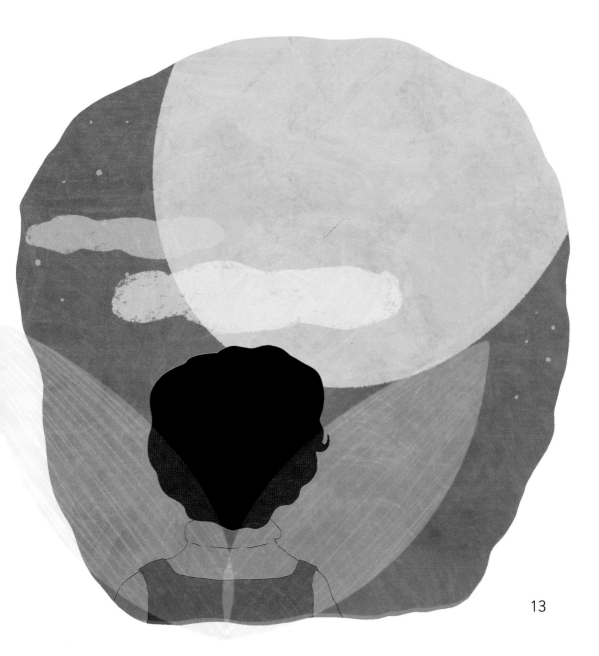

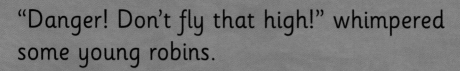

"Danger! Don't fly that high!" whimpered some young robins.

"Danger! Don't fly that far!" whimpered some mice.

But Reese didn't give up.

The huge clouds billowed. Reese was filled with dread.

Lightning crackled around her. Then a steady wind forced her down.

Reese managed to slide back to the
ground gently.
None of the moon's glow had come with her.

"Reese!" her friends shouted. "What happened?"
"I still didn't get my glow," cried Reese.

But Reese's friends had never minded.

"You didn't give up," they replied. "You followed your dreams and that's what we love about you."

This made Reese glow with joy and pride.

Reese's glow quest

:paw_prints: Review: After reading :paw_prints:

Use your assessment from hearing the children read to choose any GPCs, words or tricky words that need additional practice.

Read 1: Decoding

- Point to the word **glow** on page 18. Ask: Where does this glow come from? (*the moon*) Turn to page 21 and point to the word **glow**. Ask: Where did Reese get her glow from? (*pride and joy*)
- Focus on the different sounds made by "ou" and "y". Ask the children to sound out the following.

   young   **clouds**   **around**   **fly**   **steady**   **my**   **gently**

- Challenge the children to work in pairs and take turns to point to a word for the other to read aloud. Say: Can you blend in your head when you read these words?

Read 2: Prosody

- Challenge the children to work in groups of four to prepare a dramatic reading of pages 16 and 17.
- Ask them to think about which words to emphasise. (e.g. **forced** on page 17 – *to show the power of the wind*) and the tone to use (e.g. a deep tone for **dread** on page 16 – *to show her fear*).
- Let the groups read their pages and encourage positive feedback.

Read 3: Comprehension

- Ask the children to describe any fairies in other stories they have read. Ask: In what ways were they the same or different to Reese and her friends?
- Reread pages 20 and 21. Ask: What made Reese glow with **joy and pride**? (e.g. *her friends' praise and love*) Discuss why her friends might think following dreams is a lovable thing. Do the children agree?
- Discuss the effect of repeated words and phrases.
   o Ask: What phrase is repeated through the book? (*Reese/she didn't give up*)
   o Ask: Why do you think the author chose to repeat this phrase? (e.g. *to emphasise the number of times Reese tried to find her glow but didn't give up*)
   o Turn to page 14. Discuss why phrases are repeated. (e.g. *to emphasise how dangerous it was to go high; to increase the drama/suspense*)
- Turn to pages 22–23 and invite the children to retell the story in their own words using the pictures as prompts.